NICK BUTTERWORTH AND MICK INKPEN

STORIES JESUS TOLD

To help people understand what God is like,
Jesus told lots of stories which are as exciting
today as when they were first heard.

The Two Sons is still a great favourite
and its message is one that children especially
love to hear.

Marshall Pickering
An Imprint of HarperCollins*Publishers*
77–85 Fulham Palace Road,
Hammersmith, London W6 8JB, UK
5 7 9 10 8 6 4

First published by Marshall Morgan & Scott in 1986
This edition published in 1994 by Marshall Pickering

A catalogue record for this book is available
from The British Library

0-551-02871-8

Printed in Hong Kong

The Two Sons

Nick Butterworth and Mick Inkpen

Marshall Pickering
An Imprint of HarperCollins*Publishers*

Here is a man.
He grows apples in an orchard.

The apples are red and rosy.
It is time for them to be picked.

At home the man has two sons.

'I want you to help me to pick the apples' says the man to his first son.
'No,' says the first son.
'I'm busy.'

But after a while he is sorry
for what he said.
He picks up a basket and goes
to the orchard.

The man finds his second son.
'I want you to help me pick
the apples too,' he says.

'Yes,' says the second son.
'I will come as soon as I have
put on my boots.'

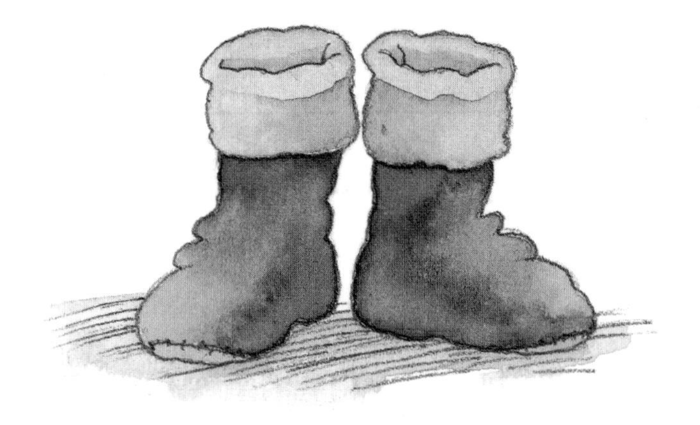

Back in the orchard the first son is busy picking apples. Look, he has already filled one basket.

‘Well done son,’ says the man.
‘Here is another basket.
We’ll have this done in no time.’

They work together until all
the apples have been picked.
But there is no sign of the
second son.
He has forgotten his promise.

Who do you think pleased his father?
The first son or the second son?

Jesus says,
‘What we do is
more important
than what
we say.’

You can read the story of **The Two Sons** in Matthew chapter 21 verses 28 to 32.

Other titles in the **Stories Jesus Told** *series*
by Nick Butterworth and Mick Inkpen

The House On The Rock
The Lost Sheep
The Precious Pearl